To

Justin McKenzie

From

Lucy Samuels

Date

11 / 18 / 17

PARABLE KIDS

A Kid's Book
of
Devotions

Kindness

31 Daily Devotions

Parable Kids
3563 Empleo
St. San Luis Obispo, CA 93401

The quoted ideas expressed in this book (but not Scripture verses) are not, in all cases, exact quotations, as some have been edited for clarity and brevity. In all cases, the author has attempted to maintain the speaker's original intent. In some cases, quoted material for this book was obtained from secondary sources, primarily print media. While every effort was made to ensure the accuracy of these sources, the accuracy cannot be guaranteed. For additions, deletions, corrections, or clarifications in future editions of this text, please write Parable Kids.

New Century Version®. (NCV) Copyright © 1987, 1988, 1991 by Word Publishing, a division of Thomas Nelson, Inc. All rights reserved. Used by permission.

International Children's Bible®, New Century Version®. (ICB) Copyright © 1986, 1988, 1999 by Tommy Nelson™, a division of Thomas Nelson, Inc. All rights reserved. Used by permission.

The Holman Christian Standard Bible™ (HCSB) Copyright © 1999, 2000, 2001 by Holman Bible Publishers. Used by permission.

The Holy Bible, New International Version®. (NIV) Copyright © 1973, 1978, 1984 International Bible Society. Used by permission of Zondervan. All rights reserved.

The Holy Bible. New Living Translation (NLT) copyright © 1996 Tyndale Charitable Trust. Used by permission of Tyndale House Publishers.

Cover Design by Kim Russell / Wahoo Designs
Page Layout by Bart Dawson

ISBN-13 978-1-58334-465-1

ISBN-10 1-58334-465-9

Printed in the United States of America

A Kid's Book
of
Devotions

Kindness

31 Daily Devotions

Table of Contents

We must not become tired of doing good.
We will receive our harvest of eternal life
at the right time. We must not give up!
—

Galatians 6:9 ICB

A Message for Parents

If your child's bookshelf is already spilling over with a happy assortment of good books for kids, congratulations—that means you're a thoughtful parent who understands the importance of reading to your child.

This little book is an important addition to your child's library. It is intended to be read by Christian parents to their young children. The text contains 31 brief chapters, one for each day of the month. Each chapter consists of a Bible verse, a brief story or lesson, kid-friendly quotations from notable Christian thinkers, a tip for kids, a tip for parents, and a prayer. Every chapter examines a different aspect of an important Biblical theme: kindness.

For the next 31 days, take the time to read one chapter each night to your child, and then spend a few moments talking about the chapter's meaning. By the end of the month, you will have had 31 different opportunities to share God's wisdom with your son or daughter, and that's good . . . very good.

If you have been touched by God's love and His grace, then you know the joy that He has brought into your own life. Now it's your turn to share His message with the boy or girl whom He has entrusted to your care. Happy reading! And may God richly bless you and your family now and forever.

Chapter 1

Kindness
Starts with You!

We must not become tired of doing good.
We will receive our harvest
of eternal life at the right time.
We must not give up!
Galatians 6:9 ICB

If you're waiting for other people to be nice to you before you're nice to them, you've got it backwards. Kindness starts with you! You see, you can never control what other people will say or do, but you can control your own behavior.

The Bible tells us that we should never stop doing good deeds as long as we live. Kindness is God's way, and it should be our way, too. Starting now!

He who sows courtesy
reaps friendship,
and he who plants kindness
gathers love.

St. Basil the Great

Faith never asks whether good works
are to be done, but has done them
before there is time to ask the question,
and it is always doing them.

Martin Luther

As you're rushing through life,
take time to stop a moment,
look into people's eyes,
say something kind,
and try to make them laugh!

Barbara Johnson

When you launch an act of kindness out into the crosswinds of life, it will blow kindness back to you.

—

Dennis Swanberg

A Kid's Tip

Kindness Every Day: Kindness should be part of our lives every day, not just on the days when we feel good. Don't try to be kind some of the time, and don't try to be kind to some of the people you know. Instead, try to be kind all of the time, and try to be kind to all the people you know. Remember, the Golden Rule starts with you!

A Parent's Tip

Your children will learn how to treat others by watching you (not by listening to you!). Acts of kindness speak louder than words.

A Prayer for Today

Dear Lord, help me
to remember that it is always
my job to treat others with
kindness and respect.
Make the Golden Rule
my rule and make Your Word
my guidebook for the way
I treat other people.
Amen

Chapter 2

The Rule That's Golden

Do for other people the same things
you want them to do for you.

Matthew 7:12 ICB

Some rules are easier to understand than they are to live by. Jesus told us that we should treat other people in the same way that we would want to be treated: that's the Golden Rule. But sometimes, especially when we're tired or upset, that rule is very hard to follow.

Jesus wants us to treat other people with respect, love, kindness, and courtesy. When we do, we make our families and friends happy . . . and we make our Father in heaven very proud. So if you're wondering how to treat someone else, ask the person you see every time you look into the mirror. The answer you receive will tell you exactly what to do.

Let no one ever come to you without
leaving better and happier.
Be the living expression of
God's kindness: kindness in your face,
kindness in your eyes,
kindness in your smile.

Mother Teresa

Anything done for another
is done for oneself.

Pope John Paul II

We should behave to our friends as we
would wish our friends to behave to us.

Aristotle

The Golden Rule starts at home, but it should never stop there.

Marie T. Freeman

A Kid's Tip

How would you feel? When you're trying to decide how to treat another person, ask yourself this question: "How would I feel if somebody treated me that way?" Then, treat the other person the way that you would want to be treated.

A Parent's Tip

Make Sure That Your Rule Is Golden, Too: Kids imitate parents, so act accordingly! The best way for your child to learn the Golden Rule is by example . . . your example!

A Prayer for Today

Dear Lord, help me always
to do my very best to treat
others as I wish to be treated.
The Golden Rule is Your rule,
Father; let me also
make it mine.
Amen

Chapter 3

Kind Words

When you talk, do not say harmful
things. But say what people need—
words that will help them
become stronger. Then what you say
will help those who listen to you.

Ephesians 4:29 ICB

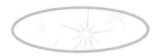

Do you like for people to say kind words to you? Of course you do! And that's exactly how other people feel, too. That's why it's so important to say things that make people feel better, not worse.

Your words can help people . . . or not. Make certain that you're the kind of person who says helpful things, not hurtful things. And, make sure that you're the kind of person who helps other people feel better about themselves, not worse.

Everybody needs to hear kind words, and that's exactly the kind of words they should hear from you!

Words. Do you fully understand their power? Can any of us really grasp the mighty force behind the things we say? Do we stop and think before we speak, considering the potency of the words we utter?

Joni Eareckson Tada

Attitude and the spirit in which we communicate are as important as the words we say.

Charles Stanley

We will always experience regret when we live for the moment and do not weigh our words and deeds before we give them life.

Lisa Bevere

Fill the heart with the love of Christ so that only truth and purity can come out of the mouth.

Warren Wiersbe

A Kid's Tip

If you can't think of something nice to say . . . don't say anything. It's better to say nothing than to hurt someone's feelings.

A Parent's Tip

Words, words, words . . . are important, important, important! And, some of the most important words you will ever speak are the ones that your children hear. So whether or not you are talking directly to your kids, choose your words carefully.

A Prayer for Today

Dear Lord, You hear every word that I say. Help me remember to speak words that are honest, kind, and helpful.
Amen

Chapter 4

It Starts in the Heart

*Blessed are the pure of heart,
for they will see God.*
Matthew 5:8 NIV

Where does kindness start? It starts in our hearts and works its way out from there. Jesus taught us that a pure heart is a wonderful blessing. It's up to each of us to fill our hearts with love for God, love for Jesus, and love for all people. When we do, we are blessed.

Do you want to be the best person you can be? Then invite the love of Christ into your heart and share His love with your family and friends. And remember that lasting love always comes from a pure heart . . . like yours!

The God who dwells in heaven
is willing to dwell also in the heart
of the humble believer.
Warren Wiersbe

The health of anything—whether
a garden plant or a heart devoted
to God—reflects what is going on
(or not going on!) underground.
Elizabeth George

The mind is a faculty,
and a magnificent one at that.
But the heart is the dwelling place
of our true beliefs.
John Eldredge

Our actions are
seen by people,
but our motives are
monitored by God.

—

Franklin Graham

A Kid's Tip

Learn about Jesus and His attitude.
Then try and do what Jesus would do.

A Parent's Tip

When you invite the love of God into
your heart, everything changes . . .
including you.

A Prayer for Today

Dear Lord, give me a heart
that is pure. Let me live by
Your Word and trust
in Your Son today
and forever.
Amen

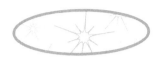

Chapter 5

Be Gentle

Pleasant words are like
a honeycomb.
They make a person
happy and healthy.
Proverbs 16:24 ICB

The Bible says that using gentle words is helpful and using cruel words is not. But sometimes, especially when we're frustrated or angry, our words and our actions may not be so gentle. Sometimes, we may say things or do things that are unkind or hurtful to others. When we do, we're wrong.

So the next time you're tempted to strike out in anger, don't. And if you want to help your family and friends, remember that gentle words are better than harsh words and good deeds are better than the other kind. Always!

If a lion's roar isn't getting you any place,
try a bear hug.

Anonymous

God has a gentle side that we need.
Some of us need it because
we've only known harshness from
the "big people" in our lives.

Bill Hybels

I choose gentleness. Nothing is won
by force. I choose to be gentle.
If I raise my voice may it be only
in praise. If I clench my fist,
may it be only in prayer.
If I make a demand,
may it be only of myself.

Max Lucado

Nothing is so strong as gentleness; nothing is so gentle as real strength.

—

St. Francis de Sales

A Kid's Tip

Count to ten . . . and keep counting: If you're mad at someone, don't say the first thing that comes to your mind and don't strike out in anger. Instead, catch your breath and start counting until you are once again in control of your temper. If you get to a million and you're still counting, go to bed! You'll feel better in the morning.

A Parent's Tip

You set a good example for your children when you follow the advice of John Baillie: "Let Christ be formed in me, and let me learn of him all lowliness of heart, all gentleness of bearing, all modesty of speech, all helpfulness of action, and promptness in the doing of my Father's will."

A Prayer for Today

Dear Lord, help me to keep
away from angry thoughts
and angry people.
And if I am tempted to have
a temper tantrum, help me to
calm down before I do.
Amen

Chapter 6

Telling Tales

A person who gossips
ruins friendships.
Proverbs 16:28 ICB

D o you know what gossip is? It's when we say bad things about people who are not around. When we gossip, we hurt others and we hurt ourselves. That's why the Bible tells us that gossip is wrong.

Sometimes, it's tempting to say bad things about people, and when we do, it makes us feel important . . . for a while. But, after a while, the bad things that we say come back to hurt us, and, of course, they hurt other people, too.

So if you want to be a kind person and a good friend, don't gossip . . . and don't listen to people who do.

Go to church to pray, not gossip.

St. Boniface of Mainz

We must be honest with ourselves
and with God. Tell God how you feel;
He knows anyway, but it will do you
good to be open and honest with Him.
Maintaining a pious façade when you
are hurting deeply only makes
the hurt worse.

Warren Wiersbe

Honesty has a beautiful and refreshing
simplicity about it. No ulterior motives.
No hidden meanings. As honesty
and integrity characterize our lives,
there will be no need
to manipulate others.

Charles Swindoll

Never utter in your neighbor's absence what you wouldn't say in his presence.

—

Mary Magdalene di Pazzi

A Kid's Tip

Watch what you say: Don't say something behind someone's back that you wouldn't say to that person directly.

A Parent's Tip

Discuss the importance of honesty with your children. Teach the importance of honesty every day, and, if necessary, use words.

A Prayer for Today

Dear Lord, I know that I have
influence on many people . . .
make me an influence for good.
And let the words that
I speak today be worthy
of the One who has
saved me forever.
Amen

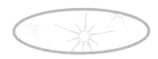

Chapter 7

Paul and His Friends

*I thank my God every time
I remember you.*
Philippians 1:3 NIV

In his letter to the Philippians, Paul wrote to his distant friends saying that he thanked God every time he remembered them. We, too, should thank God for the family and friends He has brought into our lives.

Today, let's give thanks to God for all the people who love us, for brothers and sisters, parents and grandparents, aunts and uncles, cousins, and friends. And then, as a way of thanking God, let's obey Him by being especially kind to our loved ones. They deserve it, and so does He.

I have found that the closer I am
to the godly people around me,
the easier it is for me to live
a righteous life because
they hold me accountable.

John MacArthur

When children become adults,
they remember the little things you
did together, like playing ball,
roasting marshmallows, or hiking a trail.
They rarely remember toys.

Barbara Johnson

God often keeps us on the path
by guiding us through the counsel
of friends and trusted
spiritual advisors.

Bill Hybels

Yes, the Spirit was sent to be our Counselor. Yes, Jesus speaks to us personally. But often he works through another human being.

—

John Eldredge

A Kid's Tip

The mailman can help: If you have friends or relatives who are far away, send them letters or drawings (your mom or dad will be happy to mail them for you). Everybody loves to receive mail, and so will your family members and friends.

A Parent's Tip

Think about the mentors who have had a positive impact on your own life. Then think about ways you can be a positive influence on your children.

A Prayer for Today

Dear Lord, thank You for
my family and my friends.
Let me show kindness to all
of them: those who are here
at home and those who are
far away. Then, my family and
friends will know that
I remember them and love
them, today and every day.
Amen

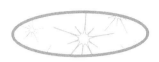

Chapter 8

When You're Angry

A foolish person loses his temper.
But a wise person controls his anger.
Proverbs 29:11 ICB

Temper tantrums are so silly. And so is pouting. So, of course, is whining. When we lose our tempers, we say things that we shouldn't say, and we do things that we shouldn't do. Too bad!

The Bible tells us that it is foolish to become angry and that it is wise to remain calm. That's why we should learn to control our tempers before our tempers control us.

When you strike out in anger,
you may miss the other person,
but you will always hit yourself.
Jim Gallery

When you lose your temper . . .
you lose.
Criswell Freeman

Anger unresolved
will only bring you woe.
Kay Arthur

No one heals himself by wounding another.

—

St. Ambrose

A Kid's Tip

No more temper tantrums! If you think you're about to throw a tantrum, slow down, catch your breath, and walk away if you must. It's better to walk away than it is to strike out in anger.

A Parent's Tip

Remember: When you lose your temper . . . you lose.

A Prayer for Today

Dear Lord, I can be so impatient, and I can become so angry. Calm me down, Lord, and make me a patient, forgiving Christian. Just as You have forgiven me, let me forgive others so that I can follow the example of Your Son. Amen

Chapter 9

When People Can't Help Themselves

I tell you the truth, whatever you did
for one of the least of these brothers
of mine, you did for me.

Matthew 25:40 NIV

Perhaps you have lots of advantages. Some people don't. Perhaps you have the benefit of a loving family, a strong faith in God, and three good meals each day. Some people don't. Perhaps you were lucky enough to be born into a country where people are free. Some people weren't.

Jesus instructed us to care for those who can't care for themselves, wherever they may be. And, when we do something nice for someone in need, we have also done a good deed for our Savior. So today, look for someone who needs your help, and then do your best to help him or her. God is watching and waiting. The next move is yours.

Reach out and care for someone who
needs the touch of hospitality.
The time you spend caring today will be
a love gift that will blossom into
the fresh joy of God's Spirit
in the future.

Emilie Barnes

Before you can dry another's tears,
you too must weep.

Barbara Johnson

I never look at the masses as
my responsibility. I look at the individual.
I can love only one person at a time.
I can feed only one person at a time.
Just one, one, one. You get closer
to Christ by coming closer to each other.

Mother Teresa

No one stands taller
in the climb to success
than when he bends over
to help up someone else.

—

John Maxwell

A Kid's Tip

When am I old enough to start giving?
If you're old enough to understand these
words, you're old enough to start giving
to your church and to those who are less
fortunate than you. If you're not sure
about the best way to do it, ask your
parents!

A Parent's Tip

Someone very near you may need a
helping hand or a kind word, so keep your
eyes open, and look for people who need
your help, whether at home, at church,
or at school. Remember that your kids
are watching.

A Prayer for Today

Dear Lord, You have given me so many blessings. Make me a cheerful, generous giver, Lord, as I share the blessings that You first shared with me. Amen

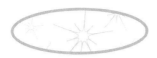

Chapter 10

How to Be Happy

Those who want to do right more than
anything else are happy.
Matthew 5:6 ICB

Do you want to be happy? Here are some things you should do: Love God and His Son, Jesus; obey the Golden Rule; and always try to do the right thing. When you do these things, you'll discover that happiness goes hand-in-hand with good behavior.

The happiest people do not misbehave; the happiest people are not cruel or greedy. The happiest people don't say unkind things. The happiest people are those who love God and follow his rules—starting, of course, with the Golden one.

True happiness consists only in
the enjoyment of God. His favor is life,
and his loving-kindness
is better than life.

Arthur W. Pink

Whoever possesses God is happy.

St. Augustine

True happiness and contentment cannot
come from the things of this world.
The blessedness of true joy is
a free gift that comes only from
our Lord and Savior, Jesus Christ.

Dennis Swanberg

People are just about as happy as they make up their minds to be.

—

Abraham Lincoln

70

A Kid's Tip

Sometimes Happy, Sometimes Not: Even if you're a very good person, you shouldn't expect to be happy all the time. Sometimes, things will happen to make you sad, and it's okay to be sad when bad things happen to you or to your friends and family. But remember: through good times and bad, you'll always be happier if you obey the rules of your Father in heaven. So obey them!

A Parent's Tip

Contentment comes, not from your circumstances or your possessions, but from your attitude. And remember this: Peace with God is the foundation of a contented life and a contented family.

A Prayer for Today

Dear Lord, make me the kind of
Christian who earns happiness
by doing the right thing.
When I obey Your rules,
Father, I will find the joy
that You have in store for me.
Let me find Your joy, Lord,
today and always.
Amen

Justin

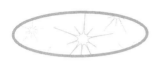

Chapter 11

What James Said

This royal law is found in the Scriptures:
"Love your neighbor as yourself."
If you obey this law,
then you are doing right.
James 2:8 ICB

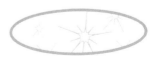

James was the brother of Jesus and a leader of the early Christian church. In a letter that is now a part of the New Testament, James reminded his friends of a "royal law." That law is the Golden Rule.

When we treat others in the same way that we wish to be treated, we are doing the right thing. James knew it and so, of course, did his brother Jesus. Now we should learn the same lesson: it's nice to be nice; it's good to be good; and it's great to be kind.

God loves these people too. Just because they're unattractive or warped in their thinking doesn't mean the Lord doesn't love them. And if we don't take them, who is going to take them?

Ruth Bell Graham

After the forgiving comes laughter, a deeper love—and further opportunities to forgive.

Ruth Bell Graham

We have the Lord, but He Himself has recognized that we need the touch of a human hand. He Himself came down and lived among us as a man. We cannot see Him now, but blessed be the tie that binds human hearts in Christian love.

Vance Havner

There is nothing that
makes us love someone
so much as
praying for them.

William Law

A Kid's Tip

Kind is as kind does: In order to be a kind person, you must do kind things. Thinking about them isn't enough. So get busy! Your family and friends need all the kindness they can get!

A Parent's Tip

Your children will learn how to treat others by watching you (not by listening to you!). Acts of kindness speak louder than words.

A Prayer for Today

Dear Lord, it's easy to be kind
to some people and difficult
to be kind to others.
Let me be kind to all people so
that I might follow in
the footsteps of Your Son.
Amen

Chapter 12

Making Other People Feel Better!

*Let us think about each other
and help each other to show love
and do good deeds.*
Hebrews 10:24 ICB

When other people are sad, what can we do? We can do our best to cheer them up by showing kindness and love.

The Bible tells us that we must care for each other, and when everybody is happy, that's an easy thing to do. But, when people are sad, for whatever reason, it's up to us to speak a kind word or to offer a helping hand.

Do you know someone who is discouraged or sad? If so, perhaps it's time to take matters into your own hands. Think of something you can do to cheer that person up . . . and then do it! You'll make two people happy.

The Christian life has two different
dimensions: faith toward God
and love toward men.
You cannot separate the two.

Warren Wiersbe

No matter how crazy or nutty your life
has seemed, God can make something
strong and good out of it.
He can help you grow wide branches
for others to use as shelter.

Barbara Johnson

Encouraging others means helping people,
looking for the best in them,
and trying to bring out their
positive qualities.

John Maxwell

Encouragement is the oxygen of the soul.

—

John Maxwell

A Kid's Tip

Cheering someone up without saying a word: If you want to cheer someone up but can't think of something to say or do, try drawing a picture or writing a note.

A Parent's Tip

Encouragement 101: Take every opportunity to teach your children ways to encourage other people. And, while you're at it, make your own home an oasis of encouragement in a difficult world.

A Prayer for Today

Dear Lord, make me a loving,
encouraging Christian.
And, let my love for Jesus be
reflected through the kindness
that I show to those who need
the healing touch of
the Master's hand.
Amen

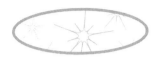

Chapter 13

Being Kind to Parents

Honor your father and your mother.
Exodus 20:12 ICB

We love our parents so very much, but sometimes, we may take them for granted. When we take them "for granted," that means that we don't give them the honor and respect they deserve.

The Bible tells us to honor our parents. That's God's rule, and it's also the best way to live. When we treat our parents with the respect they deserve, we show them that we appreciate all they have done for us. And that's so much better than taking our parents for granted, and if you don't believe it, just ask them!

We can talk about faith,
but what we live shows the true faith
behind the words.
Jay Kesler

If you are willing to honor a person
out of respect for God, you can be
assured that God will honor you.
Beth Moore

Let us look upon our children;
let us love them and train them
as children of the covenant
and children of the promise.
These are the children of God.
Andrew Murray

Parents can tell but never teach until they practice what they preach.

—

Anonymous

A Kid's Tip

Two magic words: Thank you! Your parents will never become tired of hearing those two little words. And while you're at it, try three more: "I love you!"

A Parent's Tip

Be a parent first and a friend second. As your child grows into adulthood, you'll be tempted to become "one of the boys" (or girls). Resist that temptation. Remember that your kid has lots of friends but only a couple of parents. So whatever you do, don't abandon your paternal responsibilities . . . your kid needs a parent more than a pal.

A Prayer for Today

Dear Lord, make me respectful
and thankful. Let me give honor
and love to my parents,
and let my behavior be pleasing
to them . . . and to You.
Amen

Chapter 14

Cheerfulness Now

A happy heart is like a continual feast.
Proverbs 15:15 NCV

What is a continual feast? It's a little bit like a non-stop birthday party: fun, fun, and more fun! The Bible tells us that a cheerful heart can make life like a continual feast, and that's something worth working for.

Where does cheerfulness begin? It begins inside each of us; it begins in the heart. So today and every day, let's be thankful to God for His blessings, and let's show our thanks by sharing good cheer wherever we go. This old world needs all the cheering up it can get . . . and so do we!

Christ can put a spring in your step
and a thrill in your heart.
Optimism and cheerfulness
are products of knowing Christ.

Billy Graham

The greatest honor you can give
Almighty God is to live gladly
and joyfully because of
the knowledge of His love.

Juliana of Norwich

We may run, walk, stumble, drive, or fly,
but let us never lose sight
of the reason for the journey,
or miss a chance to see a rainbow
on the way.

Gloria Gaither

Leave sadness to those in the world. We who work for God should be lighthearted.

—

Leonard of Port Maurice

A Kid's Tip

Cheer up somebody else. Do you need a little cheering up? If so, find somebody else who needs cheering up, too. Then, do your best to brighten that person's day. When you do, you'll discover that cheering up other people is a wonderful way to cheer yourself up, too!

A Parent's Tip

Cheerfulness is contagious: Remember that a cheerful family starts with cheerful parents.

A Prayer for Today

Dear Lord, make me
a cheerful Christian. Today,
let me celebrate my blessings
and my life; let me be quick to
smile and slow to become angry.
And, let Your love shine in me
and through me.
Amen

Chapter 15

Be Kind to Everyone

Show respect for all people.
Love the brothers and sisters
of God's family.
1 Peter 2:17 ICB

Who deserves our respect? Grown-ups? Of course. Teachers? Certainly. Family members? Yes. Friends? That's right, but it doesn't stop there. The Bible teaches us to treat all people with respect.

Respect for others is habit-forming: the more we do it, the easier it becomes. So start practicing right now. Say lots of kind words and do lots of kind things, because when it comes to kindness and respect, practice makes perfect.

It is my calling to treat every human
being with grace and dignity,
to treat every person, whether
encountered in a palace or a gas station,
as a life made in the image of God.

Sheila Walsh

You can be sure you are abiding
in Christ if you are able to have
a Christlike love toward the people that
irritate you the most.

Vonette Bright

When we do little acts of kindness
that make life more bearable
for someone else, we are walking in love
as the Bible commands us.

Barbara Johnson

What is your focus today? Joy comes when it is Jesus first, others second . . . then you.

—

Kay Arthur

A Kid's Tip

Respecting all kinds of people: Make sure that you show proper respect for everyone, even if that person happens to be different from you. It's easy to make fun of people who seem different . . . but it's wrong.

A Parent's Tip

Children form their ideas about God's love by experiencing their parents' love. So live—and love—accordingly.

A Prayer for Today

Dear Lord, help me to be kind to everyone I meet. Help me to be respectful to all people, not just teachers and parents. Help me to say kind words and do good deeds, today and every day.
Amen

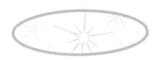

Chapter 16

Say a Kind Word

The right word spoken
at the right time is as beautiful
as gold apples in a silver bowl.
Proverbs 25:11 ICB

How hard is it to speak with kind words? Not very! Yet sometimes we're so busy that we forget to say the very things that might make other people feel better.

We should always try to say nice things to our families and friends. And when we feel like saying something that's not so nice, perhaps we should stop and think before we say it. Kind words help; cruel words hurt. It's as simple as that. And, when we say the right thing at the right time, we give a gift that can change someone's day or someone's life.

Change the heart,
and you change the speech.
Warren Wiersbe

It doesn't take monumental feats to
make the world a better place.
It can be as simple as letting someone
go ahead of you in a grocery line.
Barbara Johnson

As much as God loves to hear our worship
and adoration, surely he delights all
the more in seeing our gratitude
translated into simple kindnesses that
keep the chain of praise unbroken,
alive in others' hearts.
Evelyn Christenson

Kind words can be short
and easy to speak,
but their echoes
are truly endless.
—

Mother Teresa

A Kid's Tip

If you don't know what to say . . . don't say anything. Sometimes, a hug works better than a whole mouthful of words.

A Parent's Tip

You can guard your heart by paying careful attention to the words you speak. So measure your words carefully and prayerfully.

A Prayer for Today

Dear Lord, help me to say
the right thing at
the right time. Let me choose
my words carefully so that
I can help other people
and glorify You.
Amen

Chapter 17

God Knows
the Heart

I am the Lord,
and I can look into a person's heart.
Jeremiah 17:10 ICB

You can try to keep secrets from other people, but you can't keep secrets from God. God knows what you think and what you do. And, if you want to please God, you must start with good intentions and a kind heart.

If your heart tells you not to do something, don't do it! If your conscience tells you that something is wrong, stop! If you feel ashamed by something you've done, don't do it ever again! You can keep secrets from other people some of the time, but God is watching all of the time, and He sees everything, including your heart.

God possesses infinite knowledge
and awareness which is uniquely His.
At all times, even in the midst of
any type of suffering, I can realize that
he knows, loves, watches, understands,
and more than that, He has a purpose.

Billy Graham

There's not much you can't achieve
or endure if you know God is walking
by your side. Just remember:
Someone knows, and Someone cares.

Bill Hybels

God knows that we, with our limited
vision, don't even know that for which
we should pray. When we entrust
our requests to him, we trust him to
honor our prayers with holy judgment.

Max Lucado

The mind is a faculty, and a magnificent one at that. But the heart is the dwelling place of our true beliefs.

—

John Eldredge

A Kid's Tip

That little voice inside your head . . . is called your conscience. Listen to it; it's usually right!

A Parent's Tip

Of course we parents know that God watches over us, but we must also make certain that our children know that we know. And, we must behave in ways that let our children know that we know that He knows. Whew!

A Prayer for Today

Dear Lord, other people see me from the outside, but You know my heart. Let my heart be pure, and let me listen to the voice that You have placed there, today and always.
Amen

Chapter 18

Do Yourself a Favor

A kind person is doing himself a favor.
But a cruel person brings
trouble upon himself.
Proverbs 11:17 ICB

King Solomon wrote most of the Book of Proverbs; in it, he gave us wonderful advice for living wisely. Solomon warned that unkind behavior leads only to trouble, but kindness is its own reward.

The next time you're tempted to say an unkind word, remember Solomon. He was one of the wisest men who ever lived, and he knew that it's always better to be kind. And now, you know it, too.

The Bible instructs—and experience
teaches—that praising God results
in our burdens being lifted
and our joys being multiplied.
Jim Gallery

In a battle of wills, loving kindness
is the only weapon that conquers.
Vimalia McClure

The nicest thing we can do for
our heavenly Father is to be kind
to one of His children.
St. Teresa of Avila

Claim the joy
that is yours. Pray.
And know that
your joy is used by God
to reach others.

—

Kay Arthur

A Kid's Tip

Sorry you said it? Apologize! Did you say something that hurt someone's feelings? Then it's time for an apology: yours. It's never too late to apologize, but it's never too early, either!

A Parent's Tip

Remember that kindness is contagious; kids can catch it from their parents.

A Prayer for Today

Dear Lord, let me be
a kind person. Let me be quick
to share and quick to forgive.
And when I make mistakes,
let me be quick to change and
quick to ask forgiveness from
others and from You.
Amen

Chapter 19

The Good Samaritan

Help each other with your troubles.
When you do this,
you truly obey the law of Christ.
Galatians 6:2 ICB

Jesus told the story of a Jewish man who had been attacked by robbers. Luckily, a kind Samaritan happened by. And even though Jews and Samaritans were enemies, the Samaritan rescued the injured man.

And the meaning of the story is this: Jesus wants us to be kind to everyone, not just to our families and our friends. Jesus wants us to be good neighbors to all people, not just to those who are exactly like us.

Are you a good Samaritan? If so, you're doing the right thing, and that's exactly how God wants you to behave.

Hope looks for the good in people,
opens doors for people, discovers what
can be done to help, lights a candle,
does not yield to cynicism.
Hope sets people free.

Barbara Johnson

We hurt people by being too busy,
too busy to notice their needs.

Billy Graham

Encouraging others means helping people,
looking for the best in them,
and trying to bring out
their positive qualities.

John Maxwell

Life's most persistent
and urgent question is,
"What are we doing
for others?"

—

Martin Luther King, Jr.

A Kid's Tip

Look around: Someone very near you may need a helping hand or a kind word, so keep your eyes open, and look for people who need your help, whether at home, at church, or at school.

A Parent's Tip

Preach, teach, and reach . . . out!: When it comes to teaching our children about helping others, our sermons are not as important as our service. Charity should start at home—with parents—and work its way down the family tree from there.

A Prayer for Today

Dear Lord, make me a Good Samaritan. Let me never be too busy or too proud to help a person in need. You have given me so many blessings, Lord. Let me share those blessings with others today and every day that I live.
Amen

Chapter 20

When People Are Not Nice

*If someone does wrong to you,
do not pay him back
by doing wrong to him.*
Romans 12:17 ICB

Sometimes people aren't nice, and that's when we feel like striking back in anger. But the Bible tells us not to do it. As Christians, we should not repay one bad deed with another bad deed. Instead, we should forgive the other person as quickly as we can.

Are you angry at someone? If so, then it's time to forgive him or her. Jesus does not intend that your heart be troubled by anger. Your heart should instead be filled with love, just as Jesus' heart was . . . and is!

When something robs you of your peace
of mind, ask yourself if it is worth
the energy you are expending on it.
If not, then put it out of your mind in
an act of discipline. Every time
the thought of "it" returns, refuse it.

Kay Arthur

We are all fallen creatures
and all very hard to live with.

C. S. Lewis

You can be sure you are abiding in
Christ if you are able to have
a Christlike love toward the people
that irritate you the most.

Vonette Bright

Some folks cause happiness wherever they go, others whenever they go.

—

Barbara Johnson

A Kid's Tip

Forgive . . . and keep forgiving! Sometimes, you may forgive someone once and then, at a later time, become angry at the very same person again. If so, you must forgive that person again and again . . . until it sticks!

A Parent's Tip

Bearing a grudge = bearing a burden. You know what a heavy burden it can be to bear a grudge against another person; make sure that your child knows, too!

A Prayer for Today

Dear Lord, whenever
I am angry, give me a forgiving
heart. And help me remember
that the best day to forgive
somebody is this one.
Amen

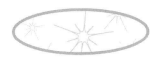

Chapter 21

Pray About It!

Do not worry about anything.
But pray and ask God
for everything you need.
Philippians 4:6 ICB

If you are upset, pray about it. If you're having trouble being kind to someone, pray about it. If there is a person you don't like, pray for a forgiving heart. If there is something you're worried about, ask God to comfort you. And as you pray more, you'll discover that God is always near and that He's always ready to hear from you. So don't worry about things; pray about them. God is waiting . . . and listening!

God makes prayer as easy as possible
for us. He's completely approachable
and available, and He'll never mock
or upbraid us for bringing
our needs before Him.

Shirley Dobson

Prayer is conversation with God.

St. Clement of Alexandria

Worry makes you forget
who's in charge.

Max Lucado

Pray,
and let God worry.

—

Martin Luther

A Kid's Tip

Open-eyed prayers: When you are praying, your eyes don't always have to be closed. Of course it's good to close your eyes and bow your head, but you can also offer a quick prayer to God with your eyes open. That means that you can pray anytime you want.

A Parent's Tip

Don't ever be embarrassed to pray: Are you embarrassed to bow your head in a restaurant? Don't be; it's the people who aren't praying who should be embarrassed!

A Prayer for Today

Dear Lord, You are always near;
let me talk with You often.
Let me use prayer to find
Your answers for my life today
and every day that I live.
Amen

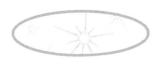

Chapter 22

Being Honest and Kind

Good people will be guided by honesty.
Proverbs 11:3 ICB

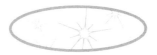

Maybe you've heard this phrase: "Honesty is the best policy." But, honesty is not just the best policy; it is also God's policy.

An important part of becoming a good person is learning to tell the truth. Lies usually have a way of hurting people, so even when it's hard, we must be honest with others.

If we are going to follow the rules that God has given us, we must remember that truth is not just the best way; it is also His way. So be honest and kind . . . now!

The single most important element in
any human relationship is honesty—
with oneself, with God, and with others.

Catherine Marshall

Those who are given to white lies
soon become color blind.

Anonymous

Honesty has a beautiful and refreshing
simplicity about it. No ulterior motives.
No hidden meanings. As honesty
and integrity characterize our lives,
there will be no need
to manipulate others.

Charles Swindoll

God doesn't expect you
to be perfect,
but he does insist
on complete honesty.

—

Rick Warren

A Kid's Tip

Honesty in Action: Thinking about being an honest person isn't enough. If you want to be considered an honest person, you must tell the truth today and every day.

A Parent's Tip

Telling the truth isn't just hard for kids. The truth can be hard for parents, too. And when honesty is hard, that's precisely the moment when wise parents remember that their children are watching . . . and learning.

A Prayer for Today

Dear Lord, sometimes it's hard to tell the truth. But even when telling the truth is difficult, let me follow Your commandment. Honesty isn't just the best policy, Lord; it's Your policy, and I will obey You by making it my policy, too.
Amen

Chapter 23

Making Friends

A friend loves you all the time.
Proverbs 17:17 ICB

The Bible tells us that friendship can be a wonderful thing. That's why it's good to know how to make and to keep good friends.

If you want to make lots of friends, practice the Golden Rule with everybody you know. Be kind. Share. Say nice things. Be helpful. When you do, you'll discover that the Golden Rule isn't just a nice way to behave; it's also a great way to make and to keep friends!

Do you want to be wise?
Choose wise friends.

Charles Swindoll

My special friends, who know me
so well and love me anyway,
give me daily encouragement to keep on.

Emilie Barnes

Friends are like a quilt with lots
of different shapes, sizes, colors,
and patterns of fabric. But the end
result brings you warmth and comfort in
a support system that makes your
life richer and fuller.

Suzanne Dale Ezell

A friend is one who makes me do my best.

—

Oswald Chambers

A Kid's Tip

First, become interested in them . . . and soon they'll become interested in you!

A Parent's Tip

Do you want your child to choose well-behaved friends? If so, talk openly to your child about the wisdom of choosing friends who behave themselves.

A Prayer for Today

Dear Lord, help me to be
a good friend. Let me treat
other people as I want to be
treated. Let me share
my things, and let me share
kind words with my friends
and family, today and every day.
Amen

Chapter 24

Sharing
Your Stuff

*God loves the person
who gives cheerfully.*
2 Corinthians 9:7 NLT

How many times have you heard someone say, "Don't touch that; it's mine!" If you're like most of us, you've heard those words many times and you may have even said them yourself.

The Bible tells us that it's better for us to share things than it is to keep them all to ourselves. And the Bible also tells us that when we share, it's best to do so cheerfully. So today and every day, let's share. It's the best way because it's God's way.

Don't be afraid to share what you have
with others; after all,
it all belongs to God anyway.
Jim Gallery

Nothing is really ours until we share it.
C. S. Lewis

The happiest and most joyful people are
those who give money and serve.
Dave Ramsey

He climbs highest who helps another up.

—

Zig Ziglar

A Kid's Tip

Too many toys? Give them away! Are you one of those lucky kids who has more toys than you can play with? If so, remember that not everyone is so lucky. Ask your parents to help you give some of your toys to children who need them more than you do.

A Parent's Tip

It's never too early to emphasize the importance of giving. From the time that a child is old enough to drop a penny into the offering plate, we, as parents, should stress the obligation that we all have to share the blessings that God has shared with us.

A Prayer for Today

Dear Lord, You have given me so much. Let me share my gifts with others, and let me be a joyful and generous Christian, today and every day.
Amen

Chapter 25

Doing What's Right

Doing what is right brings
freedom to honest people.
Proverbs 11:6 ICB

Sometimes, it's so much easier to do the wrong thing than it is to do the right thing, especially when we're tired or frustrated. But, doing the wrong thing almost always leads to trouble. And sometimes, it leads to BIG trouble.

When you do the right thing, you don't have to worry about what you did or what you said. But, when you do the wrong thing, you'll be worried that someone will find out. So do the right thing, which, by the way, also happens to be the kind thing. You'll be glad you did, and so will other people!

When we do what is right,
we have contentment, peace,
and happiness.

Beverly LaHaye

As you walk by faith, you live
a righteous life, for righteousness is
always by faith.

Kay Arthur

We are in desperate need for women
of faith who are willing to courageously
stand against sin and stand
for righteousness.

Susan Hunt

Carve your name on hearts, not on marble.

—

C. H. Spurgeon

A Kid's Tip

Think ahead: Before you do something, ask yourself this question: "Will I be ashamed if my parents find out?" If the answer to that question is "Yes," don't do it!

A Parent's Tip

Your children will learn about life from many sources; the most important source should be you. But remember that the lectures you give are never as important as the ones you live.

A Prayer for Today

Dear Lord, I want to be
a person who respects
others, and I want to be
a person who is kind. Wherever
I am and whatever I do,
let me be like Jesus in the way
that I treat others, because
with Him as my guide,
I will do the right thing,
today and forever.
Amen

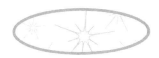

Chapter 26

Love
Your Enemies

I tell you, love your enemies.
Pray for those who hurt you.
If you do this, you will be true sons of
your Father in heaven.

Matthew 6:44-45 ICB

It's easy to love people who have been nice to you, but it's very hard to love people who have treated you badly. Still, Jesus instructs us to treat both our friends and our enemies with kindness and respect.

Are you having problems being nice to someone? Is there someone you know whom you don't like very much? Remember that Jesus not only forgave His enemies, He also loved them . . . and so should you.

Bear with the faults of others as you
would have them bear with yours.

Phillips Brooks

You don't have to attend every
argument you're invited to!

Anonymous

If in everything you seek Jesus,
you will doubtless find him.
But if you seek yourself, you will indeed
find yourself, to your own ruin.
For you do yourself more harm by not
seeking Jesus than the whole world
and all your enemies could do to you.

Thomas à Kempis

Love your enemies,
for they tell you
your faults.

—

Ben Franklin

A Kid's Tip

Making up may not be as hard as you think! If there is someone who has been mean to you, perhaps it's time for the two of you to make up. If you're willing to be the first person to offer a kind word, you'll discover that making up is usually easier than you think.

A Parent's Tip

Face facts: forgiveness can be a very hard thing to do. No matter. God instructs us to forgive others (and to keep forgiving them), period. As a parent, you must explain to your child that forgiving another person—even when it's difficult—is the right thing to do.

A Prayer for Today

Dear Lord, give me a forgiving heart. When I have bad feelings toward another person, help me to forgive them and to love them, just as You forgive and love me.
Amen

Chapter 27

His Name
Was Barnabas

Barnabas was a good man,
full of the Holy Spirit and full of faith.
Acts 11:23-24 ICB

Barnabas was a leader in the early Christian church who was known for his kindness and for his ability to encourage others. Because of Barnabas, many people were introduced to Christ.

We become like Barnabas when we speak kind words to our families and to our friends. And then, because we have been generous and kind, the people around us can see how Christians should behave. So when in doubt, be kind and generous to others, just like Barnabas.

That's what I love about serving God.
In His eyes, there are no little people . . .
because there are no big people.
We are all on the same playing field.

Joni Eareckson Tada

I have discovered that when I please
Christ, I end up inadvertently serving
others far more effectively.

Beth Moore

The secret of success is to find a need
and fill it, to find a hurt and heal it,
to find somebody with a problem
and offer to help solve it.

Robert Schuller

Do you wonder where
you can go for
encouragement
and motivation?
Run to Jesus.

Max Lucado

A Kid's Tip

Be an encourager! Barnabas was known as a man who encouraged others. In other words, he made other people feel better by saying kind things. You, like Barnabas, can encourage your family and friends . . . and you should.

A Parent's Tip

Be a booster, not a cynic. Cynicism is contagious, and so is optimism. Think and act accordingly.

A Prayer for Today

Dear Lord, let me help
to encourage other people by
the words that I say and the
things that I do. Let me be
a person who is always helpful
and kind to my friends and
family. And let them see
Your love for me reflected
in my love for them.
Amen

Chapter 28

Don't Be Cruel!

Don't ever stop being kind
and truthful. Let kindness
and truth show in all you do.

Proverbs 3:3 ICB

Sometimes, young people can be very mean. They can make fun of other people, and when they do so, it's wrong. Period.

As Christians, we should be kind to everyone. And, if other kids say unkind things to a child or make fun of him or her, it's up to us to step in, like the Good Samaritan, and lend a helping hand.

Today and every day, be a person who is known for your kindness, not for your cruelty. That's how God wants you to behave. Period.

There's a lot in the world we ought to be
very angry about: oppression, injustice,
discrimination, and cruelty
that mistreats the poor and makes
fun of the disabled.

Bill Hybels

Discouraged people don't need critics.
They hurt enough already.
They don't need more guilt or piled-on
distress. They need encouragement.
They need a refuge, a willing,
caring, available someone.

Charles Swindoll

Words. Do you fully understand their
power? Can any of us really grasp
the mighty force behind the things
we say? Do we stop and think before
we speak, considering the potency
of the words we utter?

Joni Eareckson Tada

True friends will always
lift you higher
and challenge you to
walk in a manner
pleasing to our Lord.

—

Lisa Bevere

A Kid's Tip

Stand up and be counted! Do you know children who say or do cruel things to other kids? If so, don't join in! Instead, stand up for those who need your help. It's the right thing to do.

A Parent's Tip

Do you know someone who is homebound or hospitalized? Take the kids along for a brief visit. Your children will learn that the Golden Rule requires us to reach out to those who need our encouragement and our love.

A Prayer for Today

Dear Lord, when I see meanness in this world, let me do my best to correct it. When I see people who are hurting, let me do my best to help them. And when I am hurt by others, let me do my best to forgive them.
Amen

Chapter 29

The Things
We Say

A good person's words
will help many others.
Proverbs 10:21 ICB

The words that we speak are very important because of how they effect other people. The things that we say can either help people or hurt them. We can either make people feel better, or we can hurt their feelings.

The Bible reminds us that words are powerful things; we must use them carefully. Let's use our words to help our families and friends. When we do, we make their lives better and our own.

We do have the ability to encourage or discourage each other with the words we say. In order to maintain a positive mood, our hearts must be in good condition.

Annie Chapman

So often we think that to be encouragers we have to produce great words of wisdom when, in fact, a few simple syllables of sympathy and an arm around the shoulder can often provide much needed comfort.

Florence Littauer

Like dynamite, God's power is only latent power until it is released. You can release God's dynamite power into people's lives and the world through faith, your words, and prayer.

Bill Bright

A little kindly advice is better than a great deal of scolding.

—

Fanny Crosby

A Kid's Tip

Think first, speak second: If you want to keep from hurting other people's feelings, don't open your mouth until you've turned on your brain.

A Parent's Tip

Words matter: The words you speak will help shape the kids you love . . . and once you speak those words, you cannot "un-speak" them. Even if you're not speaking directly to your kids, you can be sure that your kids are listening, so choose your words carefully.

A Prayer for Today

Dear Lord, make my words pleasing to You. Let the words that I say and the things that I do help others to feel better about themselves and to know more about You.
Amen

Chapter 30

How Would Jesus Behave?

Love other people just as Christ loved us.

Ephesians 5:2 ICB

If you're not sure whether something is right or wrong—kind or unkind—ask yourself a simple question: "How would Jesus behave if He were here?" The answer to that question will tell you what to do.

Jesus was perfect, but we are not. Still, we must try as hard as we can to do the best that we can. When we do, we will love others, just as Christ loves us.

I can tell you, from personal experience
of walking with God for over fifty years,
that He is the Lover of my soul.

Vonette Bright

We are to leave an impression
on all those we meet that
communicates whose we are and what
kingdom we represent.

Lisa Bevere

The temptation of the age is
to look good without being good.

Brennan Manning

A believer comes to Christ; a disciple follows after Him.

—

Vance Havner

A Kid's Tip

Learning about Jesus: Start learning about Jesus, and keep learning about Him as long as you live. His story never grows old, and His teachings never fail.

A Parent's Tip

How can you and your children guard your steps? By walking with Jesus every day of your life.

A Prayer for Today

Dear Lord, let me use Jesus
as my guide for living.
When I have questions about
what to do or how to act,
let me behave as He behaved.
When I do, I will share His love
with my family, with my friends,
and with the world.
Amen

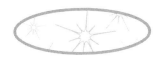

Chapter 31

God Is Love

Whoever does not love
does not know God,
because God is love.

1 John 4:8 ICB

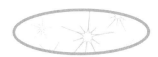

The Bible tells us that God is love and that if we wish to know Him, we must have love in our hearts. Sometimes, of course, when we're tired, frustrated, or angry, it is very hard for us to be loving. Thankfully, anger and frustration are feelings that come and go, but God's love lasts forever.

If you'd like to improve your day and your life, share God's love with your family and friends. Every time you love, every time you are kind, and every time you give, God smiles.

There's nothing you can do to get Him
to love you and there's nothing
you can do to make Him stop.

Charles Stanley

Being loved by Him whose opinion
matters most gives us the security to
risk loving, too—even loving ourselves.

Gloria Gaither

If God had a refrigerator, your picture
would be on it. If he had a wallet,
your photo would be in it. He sends
you flowers every spring
and a sunrise every morning.

Max Lucado

Jesus:
the proof of God's love.

—

Philip Yancey

A Kid's Tip

Show and Tell: It's good to tell your loved ones how you feel about them, but that's not enough. You should also show them how you feel with your good deeds and your kind words.

A Parent's Tip

Remember that God's love doesn't simply flow to your children . . . it flows to you, too. And because God loves you, you can be certain that you, like your child, are wonderfully made and amazingly blessed.

A Prayer for Today

Dear Lord, make me a person
who is loving and giving.
You first loved me, Father.
Let me, in turn, love others,
and let my behavior show them
that I love them,
today and forever.
Amen

Bible Verses
to Memorize

Love is patient; love is kind.

—

1 Corinthians 13:4 HCSB

Honor your father and your mother.

Exodus 20:12 ICB

God loves the person who gives cheerfully.

2 Corinthians 9:7 NLT

A cheerful heart is good medicine.

—

Proverbs 17:22 NIV

A friend loves you all the time.

Proverbs 17:17 ICB

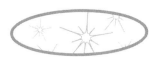

If someone does wrong to you, do not pay him back by doing wrong to him.

Romans 12:17 ICB

If I speak the languages
of men and of angels,
but do not have love,
I am a sounding gong
or a clanging cymbal.

1 Corinthians 13:1 HCSB

Now these three remain: faith, hope, and love. But the greatest of these is love.

—

1 Corinthians 13:13 HCSB

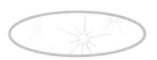

Love other people just as Christ loved us.

—

Ephesians 5:2 ICB